4/14

W9-BXE-811

MY
BIRD

Norman D. Graubart

PowerKiDS press™
New York

Published in 2014 by The Rosen Publishing Group, Inc.
29 East 21st Street, New York, NY 10010

First Edition

Book Design: Colleen Bialecki
Photo Research: Katie Stryker

Photo Credits: Cover chloe7992/Shutterstock.com; p. 5 Edoma/Shutterstock.com; p. 7 Victor Soares/Shutterstock.com; p. 9 Natalia D./Shutterstock.com; p. 11 Eduardo Rivero/Shutterstock.com; p. 13 44kmos/Shutterstock.com; p. 15 Donjiy/Shutterstock.com; p. 17 nadi555/Shutterstock.com; p. 19 Dima Fadeev/Shutterstock.com; p. 21 Vishnevskiy Vasily/Shutterstock.com; p 23 Eric Cote/Shutterstock.com.

Library of Congress Cataloging-in-Publication Data

Graubart, Norman D.
  My bird / by Norman D. Graubart. — First edition.
      pages cm. — (Pets are awesome!)
  Includes index.
  ISBN 978-1-4777-2867-3 (library) — ISBN 978-1-4777-2963-2 (pbk.) —
  ISBN 978-1-4777-3038-6 (6-pack)
  1. Birds—Juvenile literature. 2. Cage birds–Juvenile literature. I. Title.
  QL676.2.G718 2014
  636.6'8—dc23
                                        2013022503

Manufactured in the United States of America

CPSIA Compliance Information: Batch # W14PK3: For Further Information contact Rosen Publishing, New York, New York at 1-800-237-9932

CONTENTS

There are many kinds of birds. Many types can be kept as pets.

4

Cockatoos are **crested birds**. This means they have **feathers** that stick up on their heads.

7

The most common pet bird is the **parakeet**.

Birds are the only animals with feathers. Feathers make flight possible.

10

Bee hummingbirds are the smallest birds.

Cockatiels eat mostly seeds.
All wild cockatiels come
from Australia.

14

Ostriches are flightless birds. They are the largest birds in the world.

'16

Some pet birds can live for a very long time. Scarlet macaws can live to be more than 70 years old.

This house sparrow is eating a bug. Many birds eat bugs.

21

If you are gentle with your pet bird, it will be gentle with you.

'22

WORDS TO KNOW

crested bird

feathers

parakeets

WEBSITES

Due to the changing nature of Internet links, PowerKids Press has developed an online list of websites related to the subject of this book. This site is updated regularly. Please use this link to access the list:
www.powerkidslinks.com/paa/bird/

INDEX